CHIPPENHAM
AND
LACOCK
IN OLD PHOTOGRAPHS

HAROLD EVANS in Malmesbury Road at the turn of the century, possibly with one of his brothers. Malmesbury Road has changed considerably from this beautiful rural scene. It is now a very busy dual carriageway leading to the M4 motorway.

CHIPPENHAM
AND
LACOCK
IN OLD PHOTOGRAPHS

COLLECTED BY
ANNETTE WILSON AND MIKE WILSON

ALAN SUTTON

Alan Sutton Publishing Limited
Phoenix Mill · Far Thrupp · Stroud · Gloucestershire

First published 1991

British Library Cataloguing in Publication Data

Chippenham and Lacock in old photographs.
I. Wilson, Annette, *1932–*
II. Wilson, Mike, *1953–*
942.312

ISBN 0-86299-988-X

Typeset in 9/10 Korinna.
Typesetting and origination by
Alan Sutton Publishing Limited.
Printed in Great Britain by
The Bath Press, Avon.

CONTENTS

Chippenham has, at one time or another, been all things to its inhabitants and visitors. These period postcards depict it as a place for lovers or a wonderful cure for insomniacs.

THIS CARD, postmarked 2 July, no year visible but bearing a halfpenny stamp of Edward VII, shows Chippenham as an idyllic place for lovers, captioned, 'Making Hay While the Sun Shines'.

THIS POSTCARD, postmarked 8 October 1908, depicts a rather dreary Chippenham, which was in reality a bustling market town. The caption reads, 'If you're troubled with sleeplessness come to Chippenham'.

INTRODUCTION

Once *Around Corsham and Box in Old Photographs* was on the shelves, friends and acquaintances were only too happy to offer us photographs of their families, or of events which, fortunately for us, had been recorded. The result is a volume on Chippenham and Lacock.

If they had no pictures themselves, or were 'newcomers', they would suggest a visit to someone who they knew had something of interest. So, to all those people we would like to say 'thank you' all for your help and encouragement, for without you and your photograph albums this book would not be. We hope that you will enjoy, with us, looking back on just a tiny slice of Chippenham's very long and colourful history.

Some of these pictures may have appeared in one or other of the many publications put out, mainly by the Chippenham Civic Society, in the past few years although we have done our best not to use anything that has been used before. All these pictures have genuinely come from family collections, and have a personal story to accompany them.

No doubt there will be some inaccuracies, for, as with the pictures, we are dependent on the owners for the information that accompanies them and time can play havoc with the best of memories, just when you least want it too. If there are any names, dates or corrections that can be added to the information in this book, we would be only too happy to hear from you.

We would like to thank our families and friends for all their help and support during the time we have been compiling *Chippenham and Lacock in Old Photographs*.

Annette Wilson
Mike Wilson
Chippenham

Chippenham and Lacock

Chippenham has grown up in a very advantageous position, situated at one of the county's main crossroads and on the banks of the beautiful Avon. The name Chippenham is said to come from the Saxon word, *Ceap*, meaning merchandise, and *Ham*, meaning place; thus, the Marketing Place.

Before AD 800 Chippenham, with other large manors, formed part of the Crown Lands; by AD 853, it was the country seat of the kings of Wessex.

During the reign of King Alfred, Chippenham was captured by the Danes, at Christmastime in 878. King Alfred overthrew the Danes the next year, and Chippenham became the King's House once again. It was here that King Ethelwulf, father of King Alfred, celebrated the marriage of his daughter, Ethelswi-tha, to Buthred, King of Mercia.

In the reign of Edward the Confessor the people of the manor paid no taxes, but with the coming of the Normans life became very hard for the free living people of Chippenham.

By 1630, Chippenham had been deforested, and the land divided up and sold as small farms, the peasants thus robbed of their ancient rights. Over the years Chippenham has grown into a bustling market town, its houses huddled together within a wide loop of the river. Many recent changes have altered the face of Chippenham, not least the removal of the magnificent, twenty-two arch, medieval bridge which was replaced when flood prevention work was carried out in 1966.

The name Lacock comes from the Saxon, *Lacuc*, meaning little stream, this being the Bide brook around which the village has grown.

When the Domesday Survey was made Lacock belonged to Edward of Salisbury – who was then Sheriff of Wiltshire – and was valued, with its two mills and woodland, at £7.

Richard the Lionheart chose Ela, daughter of the Earl of Salisbury, to be the wife of his step-brother, William Longsword, the illegitimate son of Henry II. William became Earl of Salisbury on his father-in-law's death, and was one of the barons present when King John signed the Magna Carta in 1215. On the death of her husband Ela founded Lacock Abbey, one of the last religious houses to be dissolved in 1539. It was bought by Sir William Sharington and his successors have worked to keep Lacock in the beautifully preserved state it is today.

More recently, Lacock Abbey became famous as the home of William Henry Fox Talbot, one of the first men to discover the negative photographic process, and there is a museum to his genius in the barn next to the Abbey gates. His grand daughter, Matilda Talbot, the last squire, gave the Abbey and all her land in Lacock to the National Trust in 1944, thus ensuring that Lacock would remain unspoilt.

Locations

CHIPPENHAM BRIDGE, showing some of the beautiful eighteenth-century arches, which spanned the River Avon until 1966.

MARGARET TAYLOR, her friend Gill Brewer and Derry the dog, named after Derry Hill from whence he came, sitting on the steps of the original bandstand in John Coles Park, c. 1937.

RHODA TULLEY, née Gainey, of Langley Burrell, with her daughter Joyce in John Coles Park, in 1926. The park, lying to the west of Malmesbury Road, was named after Alderman Coles, who was three times Mayor of Chippenham. The land for the park was bought by the Borough Council with a bequest from Alderman Coles.

MR ARTHUR JAMES MOORE, for many years licensee of the New Inn in New Road, during the 1920s.

STRENGTHENING THE CHIMNEY of Hathaway's factory, just behind the railway station where the Hathaway trading area is now sited. Hathaway's made dairy utensils, including butter churns and butter workers.

THE WEIR on the River Avon, with the Monkton Hill Methodist church in the background. The weir provided the power to drive the town mill until electrically-powered machinery was installed in the early 1950s. The mill was demolished in 1958 and the course of the river has since been altered to prevent flooding.

THE OLD TOWN BRIDGE, taken from the railway viaduct. On the right side of the bridge parapet were once gates to the Borough Kennels; around twenty pairs of hounds could be kept on the island of Rea. The turnpike house can be seen, middle left. It is said that when Queen Elizabeth I was riding over the unsteady bridge at Chippenham and felt in great danger of being thrown into the river, she said, 'Oddsbodikins, these Chippenham people shall have a new bridge.' She is supposed to have given a sum of money to the bailiff, but the gift is not recorded.

THIS VIEW OF A BUSY TOWN STREET was taken in the early 1950s from the roof of the Royal Wilts, situated on the corner where the Halifax Estate Agency now stands. Many of the buildings on the left of the picture have changed: Boots the Chemists has now moved down the street to larger premises, and the dairy and the cafe have long since gone.

THE TOP OF THE HIGH STREET from St Mary Street, once called Cook Street in the late 1950s. On the left was Lennard's shoe shop, next to Melias' the grocers, followed by Milsom's gent's hairdressers and Mr Bank's fruit and vegetable shop. The corner house was, as it is today, the offices of Mr Dann the solicitor.

CHIPPENHAM MARKET PLACE was once the centre of the town; now it is just a busy junction of the A4, with the War Memorial as a roundabout. Car parking is no longer allowed in the middle of the road as shown in this picture. St Andrew's parish church towers over the other buildings, standing on the site where, it is thought, once stood a Saxon church. There is some evidence of the Norman church built into the structure of the present building. Extensive restoration work took place in 1875–7.

AVON BACK BRIDGE with River Street in the background. These buildings were all demolished to make way for a car park and supermarket, which now stands empty. The river course was altered in 1966 to prevent flooding, which regularly afflicted the town. Although the river and the architecture have changed, little boys and ducks have not; they still find water an enormous attraction.

THE LOWER END OF THE CAUSEWAY, decorated for the Coronation of Her Majesty Queen Elizabeth II in 1953. On the far left of the picture is the Jubilee Institute, built in 1887 to commemorate the Golden Jubilee of Queen Victoria.

LONDON ROAD under snow, with Chippenham District Hospital just visible on the right hand side.

CHIPPENHAM COTTAGE HOSPITAL was established in 1899 with a capacity of fourteen beds and two cots. In the same year Chippenham and Malmesbury Isolation Hospital was erected at Frogwell at a cost of £1,372, with thirty-two beds. The Cottage Hospital was extended in 1927 at a cost of £4,000. St Andrew's Hospital, the other hospital in Chippenham, was built in 1849 as an institution for the poor. It had 228 beds, roughly divided between the chronic sick and the able-bodied poor.

THIS SHOP, on the Town Bridge in Chippenham, was the retail outlet for the Hughes family's market garden at Christian Malford, and was named after their house built by the weir on the River Avon.

THE BATHING POOL on the River Avon, where the folk of Chippenham swam until the open air swimming pool was built at Monkton Park.

TAKING THE PLUNGE at Monkton Park swimming pool, built to championship standards in 1960. The pool only had a life of about twenty-five years, despite its popularity for family visits.

THE TOWNSPEOPLE OF CHIPPENHAM look on with interest as the waters of the Avon totally obliterate the arches of the Town Bridge, causing extensive flooding in the town. Major works to prevent flooding, including replacing the bridge, took place in 1966.

THE TEMPORARY BRIDGE erected across the River Avon for pedestrian use while the Town Bridge was being replaced.

CHIPPENHAM HIGH STREET under flood just before the old bridge was replaced in 1966. People are queuing on the right beside the bank, waiting to be ferried across by lorry. (The authoress may well be among them as she had to take this ferry herself to get home from work after being on duty at the Chippenham District Hospital.)

THIS PICTURE was taken from the George Inn, Lacock, after the River Avon rose twelve feet in two hours in 1935. The high pavement known as the Brash was completely under water.

THE RIVER AVON breaks its banks dramatically at Reybridge in 1935.

BILL STEVENS AND GRAHAM LIGHT, outside the village hall at Lacock, c. 1935.

LACOCK was granted a Charter by Henry III for a cloth and wool market, which was originally held in the square near the church. Lacock Market Cross was originally outside the Abbey gates and may well have been moved into the High Street when the market itself was moved into the new Market Place, the original name of the High Street. It now occupies a site which was central to the area used as a cattle market up until the eighteenth century.

Children and Schools

BETTY, PHYLLIS AND JOAN DEAN, of London Road, Chippenham, 1925.

LILA, daughter of Charles and Gladys Howard, bakers at the Old Bakehouse in Timber Street which was owned by the Miss Wilkes, c. 1925. The family lived in Dallas Road.

MADGE, Lila's sister, c. 1923. Madge served with the Women's Land Army during the Second World War.

PHYLLIS PARSONS, four years old in 1924, lived as a child in Westmead Lane, then called Factory Lane. Here she is dressed in a kingfisher blue velvet coat and dress, trimmed with white fur, with a matching hat.

ELEANOR AND ROLAND, children of Alice Holbrow.

MADGE HOWARD and her brother John of Dallas Road, c. 1928.

HAROLD EVANS in around 1912, outside number 10, but not Downing Street, although Chippenham does have one. This is in Ashfield Road, where his family lived.

CHILDREN FROM EMERY LANE at their Coronation street party to celebrate the crowning of Her Majesty Queen Elizabeth II in 1953. Back row: David and Dennis Brittain and Raymond Burgess. Front row: Rene Burgess, June Walker and Jane Taylor-Smith.

PATRICK MACKENNA, photographed by Mr Bothwell whose studio was near the Mackenna home. This photo could well be entitled, 'The Picture of Innocence'.

LOWDEN SCHOOL PLAYGROUND in 1934. The somewhat contrived nature of the photograph is due to the children having been deliberately posed, in order to show 'all aspects of play'.

FATHER CHRISTMAS in attendance at the Lowden School Christmas Party, in 1952. Christine and Jacqueline Clarke, twin sisters, are in the back row, behind and a little to the left of Father Christmas.

THE COMBINED PARISH CHURCH and Lowden Infants Sunday Schools' party in July 1920. Phyllis Parsons is seated in the front row to the right of the girl in the checked dress. The hatless man on the right of the back row is Mr Mann the caretaker of the church hall.

COUNTRY DANCE TEAM WINNERS of the Inter-schools Shield at Lowden School, 1919. Margaret Harrison is standing on the left of the back row, wearing the collar.

ST PAUL'S SCHOOL, Mr Thurston(headmaster), Miss Maud Tanner (teacher), 1923. Back row, from the left: 'Curly' Cook, -?-, ? Fenner, -?-, ? White, ? Griffin, Alan Hunt. Second row: ? Humpheries, Cyril Packer, ? Webb, ? Webb, -?-, -?-, Geoffrey Rowe. Front row: Rene Porter, Doris Holder, ? Fell, Joan Willis, Muriel Jeffries, Nelly Woodley, Evelyn Marquis, Dorothy Lovelock, -?-, -?-.

ST PAUL'S SCHOOL, taken around 1924. Back row, from the left: Joan Perry, Lily Steele, Audrey Escott, Evelyn Carvey, Ena Smith, Dorothy Phillips, Mary Hopkins, Nelly Griffin. Middle row: May Campbell, Monica Colbourne, Edith Archard, Maud Porter, Elsie Blockman, -?-, Marjorie Blake, Dorothy Emery, Phyllis Russ. Front row: Mary Baker, ? Russ, Gladys Weston, Margery Hunt, May Penwell, Rita Baker, Nancy Kilminster, Phyllis Church, Evelyn New, Lucy Cox.

IVY LANE SCHOOL, 1927. Following the changes in the education laws, the children of St Paul's School had to transfer to Ivy Lane after they were ten years old. Back row, from the left: -?-, -?-, Ernest Howell, -?-, Nelson Cole, Gerald Chapman, Rene Jones, Cecil Hiscock, Jim Carvey, Ronald Cole, ? Curley. Middle row: May Campbell, Mary Baker, Kenneth Clarke, Margery Hunt, Vera Bromley, Leonard Lovelock, Marjorie Blake, Augusta Dyer, Vera Webb. Front row: -?-, Gladys Archard, ? Fields, -?-, Mr Hinton (headmaster), Wilf Jefferies (Gaffer), ? Archard, Nancy Gough, -?-.

WESTMEAD JUNIOR SCHOOL, where the children of Mr and Mrs Dean went before attending Chippenham Grammar School. Betty became a chiropodist and Phyllis and Joan became teachers.

WESTMEAD SCHOOL, 1924. Betty Dean is sixth from the left in the second row. Miss Carpenter, the schoolmistress, lived in the Tollhouse, London Road, which has long been demolished.

WESTMEAD SCHOOL, where Mr Bryant was the headmaster and Miss Bell the schoolmistress, c. 1922. Back row, from the left: -?-, ? Wait, Dolly Webb, -?-, Gwen Roberts, ? Humpheries, Vera Davis, -?-, -?-, -?-. Next row: Tommy Woolford, -?-, Jack Franklin, Tommy Davis, ? Edwards, Granville Townsend. Sitting: Nancy Wishart, -?-, -?-, ? Woolford, Evelyn Bray, ? Brittain, ? Maloney, Lucy ?, ? Edwards. Front row: -?-, -?-, Steve Rose, ? Tucker, Harry White, Reg Wootten, -?-.

WESTMEAD INFANTS SCHOOL, 1932. Back row, from left: Joey Croft, Tom Buckland, Raymond Blanchard, Stanley Hibberd. Middle row: Donald Gough, Bertie Leafield, Margaret Taylor, Valerie Gregory, Lorna Dean, Evelyn Sparrow, Malcome Sawyer, Dennis Bullock, Donald Gough, Norman HIllier. Front row: Daphne Elms, ? Hatherell, Peter Collar, Kathleen Wheeler, Margaret Farmer, Vera Short, Rosie Hudd, Dora Gough.

BOYS OF CHIPPENHAM GRAMMAR SCHOOL, c. 1948. Jack Freegard is standing fourth from the right in the middle row; Mr Lakeman is seated centre right.

LILA HOWARD AND GORDON YEOMANS at Chippenham Grammar School in 1947. They were to
marry four years later at St Paul's church.

RUNNERS IN THE MILE RACE at Chippenham Grammar School on Sports Day 1947. Ahead in
the picture was Cavaciuti of the Waverly cafe; second, Hudson from Biddestone now living
in Australia; and third, G. Yeomans of Alderton who eventually won the race. Miss
Brooke-Evans, PE mistress, can be seen on the far right.

UNITED SCHOOLS OF CHIPPENHAM assembled for Empire Day, 24 May 1928. Among them are children in Brownie and Cub uniforms.

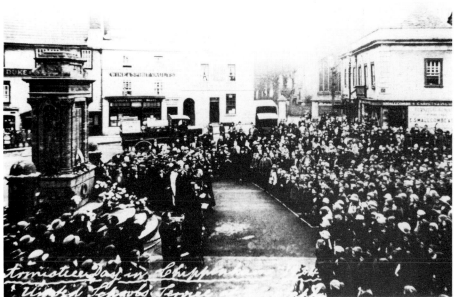

SERVICE FOR THE UNITED SCHOOLS OF CHIPPENHAM, on Armistice Day 1934, at the Cenotaph in the Market Place.

DONALD VINES, aged three, in the cottage garden at Reybridge, Lacock, in 1922.

THE CHILDREN OF THE STEVENS FAMILY at Lacock School in 1924. From the left: William, Herbert and Gladys with Eleanor in the front. There is another son, Frederick.

CHILDREN OF LACOCK playing in the River Avon at Reybridge in the stretch known as Threshold (known locally as Dresshues). All along the river there are names for different stretches. This one was called Threshold because it is the threshold of Newhall, the waterfall that ran into the Avon behind the Abbey at Devil's Hole; and so on down the river. Ken Vines is on the left, Tommy Edwards in front of Alice Cole, Fred Cole, Buster Edwards, Betty Drewitt, Edna Wicks, Ron Jones and Joan Drewitt.

GIRLS OF LACOCK SCHOOL around 1930. The headmaster at that time was Mr H. Hill.

BOYS OF LACOCK SCHOOL around 1930 when Mr H. Hill was headmaster.

LACOCK SCHOOL was erected in 1824. This picture of the school's staff and pupils taken in the 1920s includes the headmaster James Wilde on the right, and the Revd E. Moberly MA of St Cyriac's church on the left. Mr Flower, sixth from the right on the front row, still lives in Lacock today.

SECTION THREE

People

In the 1930s, an enterprising photographer based himself on Town Bridge and seems to have become one of the most prolific street photographers in the area. Though most families offered examples of his work, we include just a few. Unfortunately, we are unable to trace the name of the photographer.

MR RONALD BARNFIELD escorting his daughter Pamela past the beautiful parapet of the Old Town Bridge.

ALBERT ROBERTS, blacksmith at Westinghouse, photographed on his way home from work. Mr Roberts, who lived in 'old' Wood Lane, was employed in making signal levers.

THE SELF ASSURED YOUNG LADY pictured here, Pamela Barnfield, is still a well-known figure in Chippenham today. Now Mrs Faulkner and, until recently, a Nursing Sister at St Andrew's Hospital, she is seen here with her mother, Mrs Barnfield, on the right. This picture was taken around 1933 by the ever watchful street photographer.

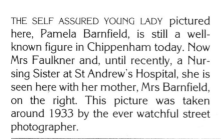

MRS LOUISA HUNT with her daughter-in-law pushing her pram over Town Bridge.

EDIE MERRET, wearing the coat with the fox fur collar, and Mrs Beatrice Parsons, wearing a brown coat and two-tone scarf, with their friend Mrs Carrington, walking over Town Bridge. The Superdrug store has replaced the buildings behind them.

CHIPPENHAM FIRE STATION STAFF outside the Yelde Hall, which used to house the fire engine, under the Bell Tower. Chief Fire Officer, Joe Buckle, was a Purveyor of Fish and Game. His shop was a magnificent Tudor building which Queen Mary visited while staying at Badminton House. Tom Millard, the seventeen-years-old Outrider, was employed as an ostler by Mr Vaughan at the Angel Hotel, before going into the Army at the outbreak of war. The fire engine horses were kept in Westmead Field, at the bottom of Factory Lane. The shop in the right hand corner of the photograph was Woods the hairdressers.

NO ONE SEEMS TO KNOW the reason for the gathering of these gentlemen. Can anyone help? Is it a club, or a reunion after the First World War, or even members of a family? The only clue we have is that Sam Weller, the licensee at the Pack Horse in London Road, is seated on the left.

MR HENRY HARRISON, his wife Ada, and their five children, photographed during the First World War. Sitting between her parents is Margaret, and grouped behind them are William, Winnifred, Constance and Thomas. The family lived in Sheldon Road.

"THE LINE OF LOVE."

MR WALTER LOVE and his wife Emily with their 'Line of Love': Walter, Emily, Alice, Ernest, John, William, Herbert, Louise, Reginald, Florence and Leonard. What a lovely photographic tribute this is to the family.

MR ROBERT PARSONS, Mr Rowland Parsons and Mr William Parsons, with Rowland's wife Beatrice, their daughter Phyllis and Mrs Alice Parsons, wife of Edward Parsons who took the photograph, in 1925. Beatrice was wearing a hat of copper-coloured straw, decorated with orange velvet flowers.

MRS ELIZA REBECCA MILLARD, who lived in Blind Lane. Her mother was born at number 31, and Eliza and her five children were all born there in their turn. Eliza married her husband Isaac, at St Andrew's parish church, and lived at number 31 all her life. The entrance to Blind Lane was through an archway beside the 'old' Borough Arms public house, which was replaced by the present building. In the fields behind the cottages, which have long been demolished, was a donkey that belonged to Mr Edwards who was foreman of the Tanyard situated beside the field. The foreman's house was below that in Factory Lane.

JOHN HUNT, master baker of Malmesbury Road, with his wife Maria and ten of their twelve children in 1912. Standing, at the back, Bert, Emma, Maria, Oscar. Beside his father is Harry. Sitting: Harold, Victor, Theodore and Norah. In the front is Edith.

VICTOR HUNT, master baker, who lived at Park-lands, with his wife Ethel and their children, Norah and Dennis, c. 1918.

MRS ETHEL HANCOCK, at the back door of her cottage at 52 Lowden, one of the cottages demolished to make way for two semi-detached houses. Mrs Hancock worked on the railway at Chippenham Station during the war; she oiled the signals and also worked as a porter. Later she worked in the sewing room at St Andrew's Hospital. She and her husband had six children; one son was killed during the Second World War, serving with the Chindits in Malaya. In the jar on the wall is a mixture of sugar and water, the country-man's wasp trap.

MR ALFRED EVANS and his wife Elizabeth, with their five children, c. 1908. Tom became a signalman for the Great Western Railway; Bert worked for Harris's the bacon company at Calne; Fred managed Wyman's newspaper stall on Chippenham Station; Wilfred was a salesman in wheat and flour for Pound Taylor and Cullins; and Harold became a train driver for the Great Western Railway.

MRS FLORENCE EDWARDS with her children, c. 1909. Standing: Millicent, Raymond and May. Centre: Joe, Maurice and Percy. Front: Archie and Reggie. Mrs Edwards and her family lived in the Sheldon Road area; Raymond eventually went to live in South Africa.

OSCAR AND LOUISA HUNT with the two eldest of their six children, Dorothy and Stanley. Mr Hunt was a master baker and had his own business in Lowden Avenue. In later life Dorothy was to cycle from Chippenham twice weekly to deliver 4-lb loaves of bread, a round trip of four miles.

TWINS LOUISE AND WINIFRED HUMPHRIES, c. 1918. Their father was chauffeur to Mr Marshall, the solicitor of St Mary Street. The girls lived on the corner of Burlands Road and Wood Lane.

DAISY GAINEY, her sister Rhoda Tulley with her daughter Joyce, and another sister Betty Beer, in a very fetching selection of Bank Holiday bonnets at Monkton Hill during the Second World War.

MR BERT TOWNSEND, Mayor of Chippenham in 1932, with his wife Ethel and their daughters, Joan and Vera. Vera was one time Carnival Queen of Chippenham.

FOUR OF THE DAUGHTERS of Mr Arthur Moore, licensee of the New Road Inn, c. 1914. Lillian is seated on the left, Gertrude and Beatrice are standing and Louise is sitting on the right. They made their own hats and dresses. They were ready to visit the Chippenham Flower Show, which was held in the field where the houses of Yewstock Crescent and Hardenhuish Avenue now stand.

RHODA GAINEY in the garden of the caretaker's cottage at Monkton Hill Wesleyan chapel, where her mother was employed as caretaker. The house has since been pulled down and a new one built.

MARJORIE HUNT with her mother, c. 1924, on the cobblestone path leading on to the island where she remembers elephants going into the river when the circus came to town.

MRS MURRAY, schoolteacher at Lacock School, together with Dinah Voss and the Revd Jeeves of St Cyriac's church on an outing to Weymouth.

WILLIAM HENRY MATON, aged two, was born at the Rose and Crown Inn. He is pictured here in 1914 with his father, Robert (Bob) Maton, landlord, in the stable yard of the Rose and Crown. One of William's earliest memories is of the circus animals in the yard; his father had let the stables to the circus owner.

DENNIS MATTHEWS was serving on motor torpedo boats. During 1940 he took his fiancée, Phyllis Parsons, to visit friends in the Service Engineers at Rowhedge in Essex.

THIS CHRISTMAS PARTY was given by Mr Edwin Self for the employees of Cocklebury Farm. It was held at The King's Head in the Market Place. Mr and Mrs Self are standing at the back of the room with their daughter Peggy and son-in-law, Brian George. Gordon Self is standing next to his mother, and in the left hand corner is Avice Wilson, author of *Cocklebury*. Mrs Summers is five back in the middle left row, beside her husband Charles; next to him is his father, John.

MR ROWLAND PARSONS, gardener to several private establishments in Chippenham and also at Frogwell Hospital and Cocklebury School, is shown here in his own garden in Greenway Lane, c. 1926. He took great pride in his tulips, Kaiser Kroom and Scarlet Emperor, which are growing in the centre bed.

MR PERCY W. BADMINTON, groom at Lackham for the Palmer family before the First World War. He served in the Northumberland Hussars and was killed in action in France on 18 September 1918, two months before the armistice.

MRS GERTIE VINES with her sons, Eric and William, outside their cottage at Reybridge in 1912.

THE VINE FAMILY in 1949 at Reybridge. From the left: Eric, Bob, Bill, Elsie, Ken, Don, with Joseph and Gertrude seated at the front.

THE VINE FAMILY having a picnic on the hills around Lacock in 1924 with Mr and Mrs Blackwell, miller for RAS Tanners of Reybridge. The others present are Mr Joe and Mrs Gertie Vines, née Church, Don Vines (on the right) and Ken Vines (on the left). Note the old iron kettle.

REG AND GLADYS BUSH of Lacock with their son Tony during the Second World War.

THE ANGEL FAMILY of Lacock Road, near the Roebuck, c. 1938. Philip Angel is third from the right.

MARTHA STEVENS came to Corsham from Wales to work for the Yockney family. She married Mr Stevens and lived in Lacock. They had five children.

MR AND MRS STEVENS, the parents-in-law of Martha Stevens pictured above, who lived in Notton near Lacock, at the turn of the century.

Churches and Weddings

JOHN SUMMERS with six of his daughters in April 1939. One of his daughters, Ella, was already married. Mrs Baker, on the far right, looks on proudly.

MRS CHARLES HOWARD at her sister's wedding.

THE MARRIAGE OF CHARLES HOWARD AND GLADYS HOUSER, on 26 June 1920. Mrs Houser, the bride's mother, is seated on the right; standing beside her is her son Frank, who gave the bride away; the small bridesmaid is his daughter. Mr Howard's best man was his brother George, the other child was a niece from Midsomer Norton, and the adult bridesmaid was Mrs Howard's friend Eva. Mrs Howard, the groom's mother, is standing to the left. Mr Howard became director of the Old Bakehouse, Chippenham.

THE TABERNACLE CONGREGATIONAL CHRUCH, now the United Reform church, St Mary Street, before the organ was installed in 1905, while the Revd J.M. Rees was pastor. The church is decorated for Harvest Festival.

A PRODUCTION OF *THE ROBE* at St Paul's Church, Malmesbury Road during the Second World War. It was enacted by members of the Tabernacle Congregational church and children evacuated from a school in Wanstead.

MARY BAREHAM OF COLCHESTER married Douglas Shipway in August 1948. The couple came to live in Audley Road, Chippenham.

THE MARRIAGE OF William Beer and Elizabeth Gainey took place at the Wesleyan chapel, Chippenham, in 1924. Elizabeth came from Langley Burrell, and William was the son of the licensee of the Red Lion, Lacock. William became the publican of The Brewery, Priory Street, Corsham, where they lived until William died, thirty-two years later.

THE WESLEYAN CHURCH, Monkton Hill, which is now the Methodist church. It was built in 1909 to replace the Wesleyan church in the Causeway, which became Spinke's Printing Works.

AFTER THE MARRIAGE of Dennis Matthews and Phyllis Parsons (seated) in November 1941. Standing, from the left: Fred and Margery Young, Jack Matthews, Margery Teagle, Florence Matthews, Barbara Chainey, Rowland and Beatrice Parsons. Taken at the home of the Matthews family.

AFTER THEIR MARRIAGE at St Paul's church, Milly and Harold Evans pose for photographs taken by Mrs Betty Huntley, Miss Gladys Ironside and 'Flashlight Willie', the only name that the gentleman on the right can be remembered by! Mrs Evans' bridesmaid was Gladys Clifford, and she wore a dress of geranium-coloured velvet and carried mauve tulips. The bride's bouquet was of pink carnations.

ALAN JEFFERIES' MARRIAGE took place at St Paul's church, with his brother Harry as best man. The Jefferies family are on the left of the picture, the bride's family on the right. May Jefferies is the bridesmaid seated on the right; Annie, the small girl seated in the front; and Richard Jefferies, the small boy.

TRIPLE WEDDING at St Paul's church, 8 April 1939. The Summers sisters, who lived at Cocklebury, are pictured with their husbands. From the front: Mildred with her husband Oliver Baker; Eileen with her husband Herbert Golding; and Laura with her husband William Whale.

DOROTHY HUNT married Walter Perry, of Mount Pleasant, at St Paul's church in the early 1920s. Walter worked at Westinghouse and his father was coachman at the Angel Hotel. This photograph was taken in the entrance to Hunt's Bakery in Lowden Avenue. From the left, back row: Florence Hunt, Mr and Mrs Perry, George Perry (best man), Maria Hunt, Oscar and Louise Hunt. Seated: Margery Hunt, Walter and Dorothy, and Winifred Hunt. The bridesmaids wore pale blue dresses, with a flower print, and the bride wore dove grey.

THE EASTER GARDEN in the baptistery at St Andrew's parish church, 1949. In 1907 the chapel of St Katherine became the baptistery. The beautiful window in the south wall is a memorial to the three sons of Dr Wilson, all killed in action in the First World War. Dominating the window are four archangels, who minister to the sorrowing. To the left are photographs of the three men alongside war scenes in Flanders. The Wilson family lived in St Mary Street.

ST ANDREW'S CHURCH CHOIR rehearsing Handel's *Messiah* under the directorship of the conductor, Mr Michael Vicars.

CANON PHILLIP SNOW taking a service at the main altar in St Andrew's church in 1973, before the pews were removed and the altar moved down into the body of the church. The changes have made it easier for a variety of activities to be arranged in the church.

MADGE HOWARD AND VIC POLLARD cutting the cake after their marriage at St Andrew's church in 1948. The cake was made by the bride's father, Charles Howard, of the Old Bakehouse.

THE CHORISTERS of St Andrew's parish church are pictured with the Revd Windsor Grace and the Revd William Reed at the wedding of Audrey Matthews and Derek Love on 26 June 1954.

CHIPPENHAM RAILWAY STATION when the guests at Madge Howard and Vic Pollard's wedding saw them off on their honeymoon.

LAVENDAR WATKINS, daughter of Rear Admiral Watkins DSO and Mrs Watkins of The Ivy, at her marriage to Captain Adam Gordon at St Andrew's parish church, Chippenham in May 1945. Alice, Lavendar's pony, drew the bride and groom from the church in a trap decorated with fruit, flowers and vegetables by her friends in the Women's Land Army. They escorted the bridal carriage through the town, riding bicycles, and holding ribbons tied to the trap.

ST ANDREW'S CHURCH autumn bazaar choir competition in 1974. From the left: Maurice Dubey, Peter Lane, Linda Hodges, Michael Gingell, James Harewood, Mark Acreman, Neil Hodges, Ian Hodges and Mr John Tomlinson, organist.

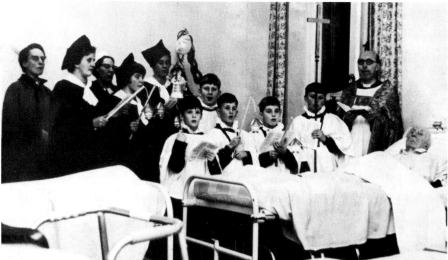

THE CHOIR OF ST ANDREW'S CHURCH singing carols at St Andrew's Hospital, Christmas 1966. From the left: Mrs Dodd (Assistant Matron), Phyllis Honour, Miss B. Swain (Matron), Susan Edwards, Jackie Douglas, Ian McMillan, Andrew Pullen, Phillip Hanover, David Lane, Simon Colebourn, with Canon Phillip Snow. We do not know the name of the patient.

THE REVD T. SUMPTER, of St Peter's church, with Miss Elsie Dudman, the verger.

ST PETER'S CHURCH SUNDAY SCHOOL, at St Peter's hall, Sheldon Road. At the back are the Revd T. Sumpter and Mr Scotford.

HARDENHUISH CHURCH CHOIR walking up to the church for a wedding. Third from the left is Mr Andrews, and fifth is Harold Evans. One of the girls was the daughter of Hawkins the builder. The church of St Nicholas was designed by John Wood and built in 1779 by the Lord of the Manor, Joseph Colbourne. The Manor House became Chippenham Grammar School.

THIS VERY HAPPY GROUP OF PEOPLE, taken outside Hardenhuish church, is thought to be a meeting of the Mother's Union, with the vicar resplendent in his boater.

PHYLLIS CLARK, with a guard of honour of friends from the Chippenham detachment of the Women's Land Army, after her wedding at Hardenhuish church in the late 1930s.

A DOUBLE WEDDING with a difference; the two bridegrooms are brothers. Gus Thatcher married Miss Doris Barnard and John Thatcher married Miss Nancy Walker, at Hardenhuish church, on Easter Monday 29 March 1937.

THE ASSEMBLED FAMILIES of the Thatchers, Barnards and Walkers, after the double wedding at Hardenhuish church in 1937. The reception was held at The Hut, Woodlands.

JACK HOLBROW and his bride who were married during the First World War. After the war, Jack became a policeman and served in Westbury.

ST CYRIAC'S CHURCH, Lacock, showing the square which was the site of the three-day fair and the original Lacock wool and cloth markets. The church itself is some 550 years old and may have been built out of the wool wealth of the area. Arthur Mee describes it as 'full of interest which those who seek will find'. Lacock has hardly changed since the invention of photography.

THE WEDDING, in 1934, of Edna Smith, daughter of the publican of The Carpenter's Arms, Lacock. From the left: Nancy Moody, Ivor Smith, Peggy Moody, Mrs Moody, Des Moody, bridegroom, Edna Smith, Jack Moody, -?-, Grace Smith, Dorothy Smith and Jim Smith. The bridesmaids' dresses were all pale green and were made by the bride.

THE REVD GILES BROCKLEBANK with HM The Queen Mother on a visit to Lacock church. When staying at Spye Park for the Cheltenham Races she always came to see the crocuses at Lacock Abbey.

HM THE QUEEN MOTHER on one of her visits to Lacock church. PC Northover is on duty on the left of the picture.

THE FLOWERS, FAMILY AND FRIENDS outside their house in the High Street, Lacock, after the marriage of Joan Flowers to Bert Homewood at St Cyriac's church.

KEN VINES married Marie at Lacock church. 'Lottie' Collins, on the right, a warrant officer serving with Ken during the Second World War, gave the bride away. The best man was William Vines and the Matron of Honour was Eleanor Vines.

Occupations

DONALD VINES, who trained to be a blacksmith, in Lacock, in 1938.

THE TOOL GRINDING SECTION at Westinghouse Brake and Signal Works. Working the machine in the front of the picture is Harold Pope. Percy Hall and Idris Lewis are working beside Leonard Cleverley, supervisor, standing on the left.

WESTINGHOUSE BRAKE AND SIGNAL COMPANY. From the top of the staircase: Fred Williams (left), Jimmy Thompson (right), Ted Jeffries (left), Bill Perry (right). The next three are unknown, and bottom right is Dick Webb.

THE DRILLING SECTION at Westinghouse Brake and Signal company. Bill Mills, Leonard Cleverley, Lesley Townsend, Joe Clifford working on single spindle drills. Mr Coates on the right is working on a four spindle drill – drilling eye rods for signal fixings.

WESTINGHOUSE BOWLS TEAM, Cup winners. Back row, from left: -?-, Dick Webb, Ted Jefferies, Fred Williams, Harry Slade, Harry Hudd, Bill Perry, -?-. Front row, from left: Cecil Hemmings, Jimmy Thompson, -?-.

THIS PICTURE, taken in 1914, appeared in *Westinghouse News*. Leonard Cleverly, ninth from the right (standing behind the man in the white overall), was section supervisor in the milling section.

WESTINGHOUSE CHRISTMAS CARNIVAL, taken just before the Second World War. Staff were entertained by a 'Gypsy' band.

A PRE-SECOND WORLD WAR CHRISTMAS PARTY at Westinghouse. Some of those present were, at the back: Harry Reckless, Arthur Tapper, Dixie Kidd, Harold Swan, Roland Angel, Archie Adams, Dazzle Cleverley, Stan Silcox and Fred Young. Seated: Moly Manners, Zelda Jones, Ivy Hill, Nelly Davison, Mr Cruse (works manager), Theresa Hill, Norah Hopkins and Dorothy Easter.

ROAD GANG working in the Sheldon Road area. Mr Harper, 'playing' the shovel, was known in the community as a 'comedian' and quite good fun. His wife was a dressmaker.

MR HENRY HARRISON, working at his bench at Downing and Rudman. Mr Harrison would be contracted out to work with Mr Brakspear, the architect, and was involved in the renovation of churches all over the country. His beautiful carvings can be seen in Chippenham parish church, in the chancel screen, and in Malmesbury and Battle Abbeys.

OLIVE BISHOP AND PAT HILL clearing up after Freeman, Hardy and Willis, the shoe shop, was flooded in 1965.

RETIREMENT PRESENTATION to Mr Albert Matthews, at the United Dairies, around 1972.

GIRLS OF NESTLE'S MILK FACTORY with their foreman, Frank Stanley. They worked in the filling room, where the cans of milk were filled by hand. The milk was poured into channels running above the benches, and came down through pipes to fill the cans held by the girls. If the men, pouring the milk into the filling pans overhead, felt like playing the fool they would sometimes 'accidently' miss the pan and pour the milk onto the girls underneath! This photograph was taken around 1910. Back row, from left: Doris Blackford, Rene Broome, Edie Watts, Gwen Barnes, Lil Dolman, Lucy George, Iris Pearson, Violet Sims and Ivy Bradley. Front row: Chris Garlick, Maggie Burchall, Mary Ferris, Eva Archard, Dorothy Noyes, Chris Sritton, Dorothy Holly, Kit Hares and ? Britton.

MILK was delivered around the area by milkfloat from the farm in Pewsham, now completely built over. In the foreground: Mr Burton, Dennis Matthews and ? Coates. As the milkfloat belonged to a W. Townsend, it is probably him standing in the second float, centre back. The photograph was taken in 1932.

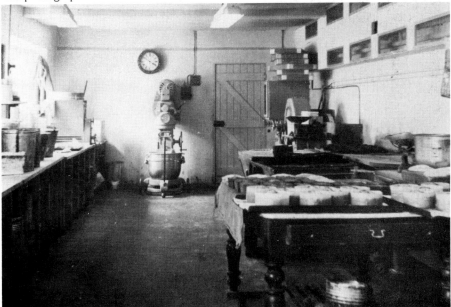

INSIDE THE OLD BAKEHOUSE, where Mr Charles Howard was director. A master baker, Mr Howard had a staff of seven people, which included an assistant baker, a confectioner and assistant confectioner. The Old Bakehouse was owned by the Miss Wilkes.

WYMAN'S NEWSPAPER STALL, Chippenham Railway Station, which was managed by Mr Fredrick Evans. The young gentleman with Mr Evans, wearing a cap and shorts, is probably a boy porter.

SWEET SHOP AND COFFEE ROOM retained by Mrs Candy after her husband died around 1954. This picture was taken during a promotion for Bassett's Liquorice Allsorts, the counter frontal is covered with a decoration of their sweets.

MISS WHITE at the door of Barrow's sweet shop, where Milly Evans also worked for some fourteen years. Note the archway to the right of the picture which is the coach entrance to the Black Horse Inn in New Road. Fry's, Cadbury's and Rowntree's were obviously the big names in the sweet business, although Barrow's were renowned for their home-made chocolates. Photograph taken c. 1930.

BAXTER'S BUTCHER SHOP, Chippenham, showing George Rice, wearing the boater, and Mr Tommy McKenna, with the staff of the shop which was situated near the 'old Post Office'.

WALTER NEALE, pictured outside his butcher shop on the Causeway. Mr Iles, who runs the same business today, would be unable to repeat this wonderful display due to modern hygiene regulations.

JACK AND HILDA MOSS in their garden at The Hamlet in the early 1930s. Mr Moss was an engine driver for British Railways.

TOM GREGORY being presented with a long service medal. Harold Evans, on the right, received the title of Train Driver of the Year at the same ceremony, some time in the early 1930s.

BILL WEBB, INSPECTOR, presenting Bert Southey with his retirement gift outside the Permanent Way Inspection Office at Chippenham Railway Station, around 1965/6. Those present were, on the left: two gentlemen from the Bristol office and Bill Crombe. At the back: station master and Arthur Ling. Centre: inspector, two more Bristol representatives, Mr Harold Longshaw (assistant sub-inspector), and Mr Fred Nash.

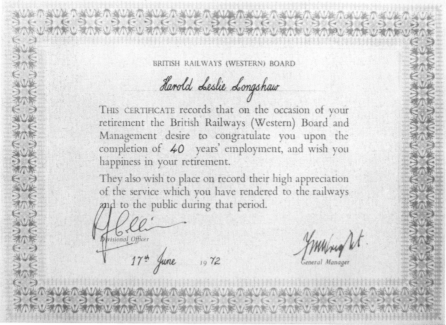

BRITISH RAILWAYS (WESTERN) BOARD

Harold Leslie Longshaw

THIS CERTIFICATE records that on the occasion of your retirement the British Railways (Western) Board and Management desire to congratulate you upon the completion of **40** years' employment, and wish you happiness in your retirement.

They also wish to place on record their high appreciation of the service which you have rendered to the railways and to the public during that period.

Divisional Officer

17th June 19 72

General Manager

MR HAROLD LONGSHAW'S retirement certificate, awarded after forty years with British Railways.

MR JACK BISHOP being presented with a clock by Mr Barnes, postmaster, on his retirement from the post office in Chippenham, 1976.

THIS THRESHING MACHINE belonged to Dick Jennings who had a garage on the Bath Road. The machine was hired out to local farmers and the Land Army girls 'went with it'!

MR ARMSTRONG AND HIS FAMILY outside the quaint cottage in Wood Lane where he carried on his boot repair business. This picture is estimated to have been taken around 1930, and, as the notice says 'Late of HMS', Mr Armstrong was obviously a retired serviceman. Sadly, the cottage was demolished some years ago.

PC NORTHOVER, second from the left on the back row, with his fellow trainees at Devizes Police College. He was village constable at Grittleton and later at Lacock.

PC NORTHOVER on duty at Lacock on the occasion of the visit of HM Queen Elizabeth the Queen Mother.

MICHAEL BISHOP on duty at the Changing of the Guard Ceremony at Whitehall. He was the son of Olive and Jack of Heathfield, Chippenham and he joined the Royal Horse Guards in 1957 when he was seventeen years of age. He also took part in the Trooping of the Colour Ceremony for the Queen's Birthday Parade.

ELSIE TURNER, now Mrs Dagger of Riverhouse, St Mary Street, in her uniform while working at Marlborough Buildings, Bath, 1925. Before that, she was employed at Sherriff's Hotel, Bath, and when off duty could walk through the basements into Parade Gardens and enjoy the 'peace and quiet'.

MR DONALD VINES of Reybridge, Lacock, a trainee farrier at Jack Ring's blacksmith shop in 1938. In order to preserve the character of the village, the smithy building has been converted into a bus shelter, next to the George Inn.

RICHARD BALL pictured during his training at Lackham Agricultural College. He was trained in all aspects of the rearing and keeping of poultry.

A VERY YOUNG JOSEPH VINES, on the far right wearing the large hat, pictured with a group of carpenters from Lacock at the turn of the century. It is not known where they were working.

SECTION SIX

Transport

'BONNIE' FREEGARD, with Champion the horse, c. 1937. Champion drew the flatbed goods delivery cart for the GWR from Chippenham Railway Station and had the reputation of being a 'nutty horse'! He was beautifully behaved in town, but as soon as they reached Station Hill he would take off and gallop like mad back to his stable, situated behind the cottages which once stood at the top of the hill.

IN THE OLD DAYS milk was delivered to the door, but not in bottles. It would come straight from the farm, in the churn, and be measured, in pints or quarts, and poured directly into your jug. The house next door to Dean's shop, the cottages in Queen's Square and the Tollhouse in this picture have all been demolished to make way for new houses.

A STEAM LOCOMOTIVE causes great interest as it enters Chippenham on the London Road, passing the Tollhouse with the old cottages of Queen's Square behind it.

MR GILFORD HUNT with his father's delivery cart, in Malmesbury Road in the early 1920s. Mr Hunt's father was a master baker and most of his family were involved in the business.

NICK BAKER, trying his hand at driving his uncle's motor cycle, behind Dean's store in the London Road.

MECHANIZATION HAS ARRIVED! Gilford Hunt with the new Trojan delivery van which replaced the horse and cart used for his father's bakery round in the early 1930s. Gilford, with his foot on the running board of the van, is accompanied by the delivery assistant, Mr Tanner. The van's number plate reads YA17.

THE HATHAWAY FAMILY off to vote on 20 January 1906. According to the campaign notice on the car, their vote is going to support Joseph Chamberlain's policy. George Hathaway, C.J. Hathaway, T.W. Hathaway and N.S. Hathaway are pictured.

MEMBERS OF THE TABERNACLE CONGREGATIONAL CHURCH pictured at Sydenham. Maybe they were visiting Crystal Palace which moved there in 1854 and was a popular place for visits, until it burned down in 1936.

THE STAFF OF THE INTERNATIONAL STORES on a charabanc outing to Weston-super-Mare. The International Stores was situated where Rumbelows is now. Note the iron wheels on the bus; in the days before pneumatic tyres they were covered with solid rubber bands.

OSCAR HUNT AND FRIEND on holiday in Jersey in 1929.

LACOCK'S WORKING MEN'S CLUB outing to Cheddar Gorge, 1939.

BILL STEVENS and Violet Baker on the Calthorpe combination, with Jack Stevens on his AJS, in Lacock High Street.

GRANNY STEVENS in the basket chair, outside the house of Mr and Mrs Bird in Bewley Lane, Bowden Hill, Lacock; the chair was kept at the rectory for the villagers' use.

Wartime

THE CAP RIBBONS worn by Dennis Matthews during his war service in the Second World War. He was transferred from HMS *Hood* just before it was lost in enemy action.

FIRST WORLD WAR SOLDIERS convalescing at the Neeld Hall, 1918. William Thompson was serving in the 6th Leicesters when he was shot in the thigh and knee. He was treated at the American Hospital in Valenciennes, after being carried for miles by German prisoners of war, who, he said, were 'real nice chaps'! Mr Thompson, who lives in Westmead Lane, is sitting first left, in the front row.

MR WALTER LOVE, right, butcher of New Road, with his sons and members of staff during the First World War. From left to right they are Leonard, William, John, Herbert, Ernest and Reginald.

GLADYS HOWARD, who drove an ambulance during the First World War and married Charles Howard of the Old Bakehouse.

ALFRED MILLARD, ? Gale of Wood Lane and George Millard of 31 Blind Lane. Just a few days after this photograph was taken in 1918, George was killed in France, four days before the First World War ended.

CHARLES HOWARD during the First World War, c. 1917.

JACK HOLBROW, on the right of the doorway, in training at Purbright at the beginning of the First World War.

HM QUEEN MARY and Lady Cooper with New Zealand soldiers who were stationed at Grittleton. At Lady Cooper's request they were entertained at Greenways, her home. A choir sang for them and Mrs Evans made mince pies. Later Greenways became Chippenham's maternity home.

SECOND WORLD WAR HOME GUARD, thought to have been taken at Greenways, the home of Lady Cooper. Among the men pictured are: Cecil Robinson, Sid Waite, Neville Marsh and Ernie Hewer.

CHIPPENHAM HOME GUARD, after exercises at the park of Seagry House, during the Second World War.

MR JOHN 'JACK' SHIPWAY and two of his sons, Douglas and Ron of the Gloucestershire Regiment, back from Japan in 1945.

THE CARD ISSUED TO BLOOD DONORS during the Second World War, thanking the donor for generously giving blood for the Fighting Forces, and with a quotation from Shakespeare's *Henry V*.

LAPEL BADGE, with the monogram of King George VI, issued to servicemen after the Second World War.

CHIPPENHAM DETACHMENT OF THE WOMEN'S LAND ARMY, whose area representative was Lady Methuen. Back row, from left to right: Margery Hunt, -?-, -?-, -?-, Betty Bailiff, ? King. Middle row: -?-, Madge Howard, Lavendar Watkins, Marjorie Hunt, -?-. Front row: Peach Kent, -?-.

MEMBERS of the Chippenham detachment of the Women's Land Army, who were the 'Gang' of the threshing machine that travelled the area during the Second World War, harvesting the local farmers' crops. From the left, as far as can be remembered, are: Flo Farmiloe of Downing Street, Chippenham, -?- from London, -?-, Bridget ? from Ireland, Len Weston from the Lowden area, Aggie from London and George ?.

CHIPPENHAM DETACHMENT OF THE WOMEN'S LAND ARMY, resting on the wall of St Andrew's church during the Victory Parade (see the decorations on the windows of the Old Vicarage). Back row, from the left: -?-, -?-, Phyllis Clark, Marjorie Hunt, Betty Bailiff, -?-. Front row: -?-, Lavendar Watkins, -?-, -?-, Madge Howard.

THREE OF THE CHIPPENHAM DETACHMENT of the Women's Land Army – Marjorie Hunt, Margery Hunt and Peach Kent. Their uniform consisted of a green jersey, khaki trousers or breeches, and a wide-brimmed hat.

AUXILIARY FIRE SERVICE TEAM during the Second World War.

AS THE SECOND WORLD WAR came to an end, many things were in short supply, including batteries. Mr and Mrs Candy received a message from Ever Ready, asking them if they wanted six gross of No. 8 batteries! At the same time Brocks offered them the first consignment of fireworks. They accepted, of course, and had to collect the goods themselves from the railway station. They sat up until well after midnight, putting fireworks into two and sixpenny packages for fair distribution, placed a notice in the window that the batteries would be on sale for 1 s. from 7.30 in the morning, and went to bed. Mr and Mrs Candy were woken very early that morning and, on looking out of their window, saw a huge queue of people waiting for the shop to open. According to the police, the queue stretched for a quarter of a mile.

DONALD SMITH, on the left, and Fred Stevens, who both served in the Wiltshire Regiment during the Second World War. Donald was one of four brothers who all managed to meet up while on active service.

CALLING THE TROOPS on to parade. Donald Vines of Lacock serving in Italy with the Royal Engineers in 1943.

CHIPPENHAM 'OLD CONTEMPTIBLES', the name given to the soldiers of the British Army sent to France at the outbreak of the First World War by Wilhelm II in 1914. Back row, from the left: J. Niblett, ? Fortune, -?-, -?-, ? Rush, ? Stevens, ? Donovan, -?-, -?-, A. Blanchard, H. Blanchard. Middle row: R. Cook, -?-, -?-, ? Thompson, A. Taylor, J. Barrett, B. Large, -?-, ? Pullin, ? Parsons, ? Reynolds, -?-. Front row: ? Lenton, B. Keel, -?-, ? Hatcher, ? Carey, ? Wood, ? Dyer, -?-, ? Hawkins, ? Hatherell, ? Fortune, ? Webb.

SECTION EIGHT

Organizations

COMMITTEE MEETING of the British Legion Club, held in St Mary Street, some time in the late 1930s. From the left: Mr Hill, -?-, Mr Sidnell, Mr Stuckey, -?-, Mr Rebbick, -?-, Mr Alf Bevan (presiding), Mr Rowland Parsons, -?-, -?-, Mr Huxtable.

MONKTON HILL GIRLS CLUB outing to Minchinhampton Common in Gloucestershire.

PHOTOGRAPHED AT THE ROYAL OAK, this is thought to be a Royal Antediluvian Order of Buffaloes occasion. The landlord and his wife, Mr and Mrs Sam Perry, are in the group. Among those pictured are: J. Allen, A.E. Taylor, ? Goby, ? Clark, C. Brinkworth, ? Griffin, ? Lundy, ? Brewer, H. Whale, ? Noble, S. Perry, ? Sims, ? Clark and ? Norris.

MEMBERS OF THE LOYALTY LODGE, Royal Antediluvian Order of Buffaloes, shortly after the First World War. Back row: C.B. Taylor, R. Fellender, A. Greenaway, J.R. Brown, G. Freegard, R. Bull, W.C. Bennett, A. Copley, H. Jeffries, W. Love, H. Pike, W. Dorsett, W.H. Porter, W.J. Witts and G. Jones. Front row: J. Althoff, H. Bennett, R. Bennett, F. Greenman, F.G. Hunt and H.G. Pinfield.

CHIPPENHAM TOWNSWOMEN'S GUILD celebrating an anniversary with an international theme, hence the dolls in costume. From the left: Marjorie Vince, -?-, -?-, Mrs Vince, Vera Townsend, Mrs G. Howard, -?-.

A MEETING OF CHIPPENHAM TOWNSWOMEN'S GUILD. Among those present were Vi Johnson, Vi Macky, Mrs Hiscocks, Phyllis Gammon, Mrs Hardiman, Mrs Gibbons, Vi McGregor, Mrs Keevil.

MEMBERS OF THE LICENSED VICTUALLERS about to leave on a coach outing. They are pictured outside Steint's shop in Station Hill. Behind the lamp is the Plymouth Brethren chapel, and next door to that, behind the tree, is the Picture Palace, where 'Martha' was the cashier. Among those in the group are Billy Wood, Oscar Hunt, ? Baker, Billy Reynolds, ? Wood, Bert Love (grocer), Mr Troughton, Mr Boulton, Mr Bill Steint, Ernie Love (butcher) and ? Wood.

A GATHERING OF MEN outside the Great Western Hotel, some time in the early 1920s. No one seems to know quite what these 'bright sparks' are up to. The board held up in the middle of the group reads, 'The Merry Lads from Chippenham, Flash Box Club Outing'. Albert Taylor, centre front with the banjo, and Mr Harris, next to him, were Post Office telegraph workers, which may be a clue, but what about the tipsy looking policeman at the back? The Great Western Hotel was demolished in 1967, when all the changes were made in the area, to make way for Bewley House.

AN 'ENTERTAINMENT', thought to be a cantata, by the Girls Friendly Society. Back row, from the left: ? Ricketts, Winnie Hunt, -?-, ? Guest, Clarice Platts, Molly Habgood, May Ricketts. Second row: Kitty White, Grace Knapp, Phyllis Paul, Edith Howell, -?-, -?-, ? Hodgson, Winnie Scott. Front row: Amy King, Edith Edwards, -?-, Eva Boulton, -?-. The name of the leader is not known.

THIS CERTIFICATE was presented to Louisa Jefferies on the occasion of her marriage to Oscar Hunt, on 24 August 1898. She had been a member of the Girls Friendly Society for nine years. The wording is from Proverbs chapters XII–XXXI: 'A virtuous woman is a crown to her husband: her price is far above rubies ...'

A NICELY ARRANGED PHOTOGRAPH of members of Chippenham Cycling Club, thought to have been taken at the rear of what is now Barret's Furniture Shop, near the Railway Arches, 1900.

RUBY GILBERT spent a lot of her childhood travelling the world with her parents. Her father was Sergeant Major Hann of the 1st Battalion Somerset Light Infantry. Ruby was five years old when they went to Egypt, then to China and Hong Kong, where this photograph of a Brownie and Guide gathering was taken around 1928. Her father was posted to India before they returned to England when Ruby was twelve years old.

CHIPPENHAM DETACHMENT RED CROSS CADETS, c. 1945. Pamela Barnfield is fourth from the left in the front row.

CHIPPENHAM YOUNG CONSERVATIVES in Corsham Park, having walked from Chippenham, in the mid to late 1930s. Not including the three young ladies in the distance on the left of the photograph, they are, from left to right: Sonia Boggett, Barbara Hall, an airman, Phyl Parsons, Nora Dunn, John Fenner, M. Hunt, Tony Hall.

MEMBERS OF THE CHIPPENHAM CONSERVATIVE ASSOCIATION visiting Mr David Eccles, Member of Parliament for Chippenham, at the Houses of Parliament in the mid-1940s. Mr Eccles is fourth from the left. To his right is Mrs May Love, with her husband Bill behind her. To his left is Mrs Larkham, and behind and to her left is Mr Bert Love and his wife Dolly. Mrs O'Halleran is on the far right.

ST ANDREW'S CHURCH WOMEN'S GUILD, 1946: 'The Girls at Cheddar'. Front row: Mrs Tanner, Mrs Taylor, Mrs Large, Mrs Large, Mrs Rudman. Second row: Mrs Jones, Mrs Hillman, Mrs Green, the vicar's wife, Mrs Down, Mrs Blanchard. Third row: -?-, -?-, -?-, Mrs Hood, Mrs Hillman.

CHIPPENHAM OLD-TIME MODERN SEQUENCE DANCING CLUB, taken in the late 1960s. Mr Warner is standing third from the left at the back, and his wife, sixth from the left. Doreen Clarke is seated on the left, and her husband, Harold, is seated on the right.

ST ANDREW'S BOYS BRIGADE, 1969. Front row, from left: Neil Hodges, Mark Acreman, Ian Hodges, Martin Harding. Middle row: Colin Hughes, -?-, -?-, Ian Guy, Nigel Guy, -?-, -?-. The leaders at the back are Derek Love and Robin Hardie.

CHIPPENHAM AMATEUR SWIMMING CLUB with their entry during the 'National Learn to Swim Year' carnival. Mrs Winterton is standing on the extreme right, and Dave Chamberlaine, the club's swimming coach, is just in front of her holding the Chippenham ASC notice.

SCOUTS AND CUBS outside the Audley Road Scout hall in 1925. Lady and Mr Coventry, of Monkton House, are seated in the centre. Next to Mr Coventry is Mr Dear, headmaster of Lowden School. Among the Scouts were Cecil Robinson, Peter Mortimore, Alan Hunt and Vince Williams.

ERIC BAKER being presented with the Cup for Best Cub by Mr Dykes, Mayor of Chippenham, accompanied by his wife. Cecil Robinson, Scout leader, is looking on.

THE COLOURS OF THE NORTH-WEST GIRL GUIDES ASSOCIATION leaving St Andrew's parish church after the Thinking Day Service on 22 February 1970. This service was held to celebrate sixty years of guiding on the joint birthdays of Lord and Lady Baden-Powell. Jenny Wilson, front left, was confirmed by the Bishop of Malmesbury, at Corsham church, that same evening.

MONKTON HILL OPERATIC COMPANY. Among those pictured are Marjory Shewring, Betty Usher, Mrs Gammon, Kath Wheeler and Eileen Whitmarsh.

LACOCK WORKING MEN'S CLUB OUTING. Joseph Vines is seated on the ground, front left.

LACOCK SCOUTS at Bowood.

DON VINES having an early morning wash at Scout camp, Bowood, pictured here with Tommy Edwards, 1934.

OVER SIXTIES CLUB, held at Lacock Oddfellows' Hall. Back row, from the left: Mrs Tom Selman, Mrs Baker, Mrs Chivers, Mrs Chamberlain, Sam Crew, Edie Ball. Middle row: Mrs Rawlings (then 102 years old), -?-, Mrs Hinton, -?-, Martha Stevens, -?-. Front row: Mrs G. Vines, Kate Vines, Mr Baker, Mrs Chivers, Mrs Edmunds, -?-.

WOMEN MEMBERS OF LACOCK CIVIL DEFENCE TEAM learning to cook with a field kitchen, in the grounds of Lacock Abbey. They are using a brick oven and a dustbin cooker, complete with stovepipe. Next to the stovepipe is Mrs Murray and Eleanor Vines; Bab Troon and Mrs James are to the right.

SECTION NINE

Sport and Leisure

THE AVONVALE HUNT at Wick Hill passing Maud Heath's monument, where she sits overlooking the Causeway that she had built in the fifteenth century. This generous lady, feeling sorry for the villagers walking along the muddy four mile track to Chippenham, had the Causeway made. This pathway is still maintained today and paid for out of the Maud Heath Trust. Apart from the monument, there is a plaque, testifying to her generosity, on Kellaways Bridge, and a stone, near St Paul's church, which says:

'Hither extended Maud Heath's gift,
For where you stand is Chippenham Clift.'

GYMKHANA held in Monkton Park in 1944. Marie Mackenna is on the right hand side of this group of riders.

VET'S WIFE MRS HALE, on the car roof, with her daughter Gillian riding Sea Trout in the early 1950s. What a wealth of old cars there are in the background. This picture should keep many a motor enthusiast quiet trying to identify them!

ST ANDREW'S CHURCH GIRLS HOCKEY TEAM matched against Ivy Lane School, 1937. Back row, from the left: Edna Tucker, -?-, Ethel Whittle, -?-, Barbara Tucker, -?-, -?-, Joan Kidd, Mr Dowse, Barbara Kidd, -?-, -?-, -?-, -?-, -?-, -?-. Middle row: -?-, -?-, -?-, Peggy Beynam, -?-, Margaret Farmer, Cynthia Weaver, Megan Large, -?-, -?-, Joan Bray, -?-, -?-. Front row: Doreen Archard, -?-, -?-, -?-, -?-, Margaret Banks, Margaret Taylor, Pearl Mizen, -?-, -?-, -?-, -?-.

CHIPPENHAM GRAMMAR SCHOOL HOCKEY TEAM, 1947. Back row, from the left: Lucy Reece, Audrey Grimes, -?-, -?-, -?-, Mary Farrer, Margaret Young, Jean Sharp. Front row: Audrey MacKeowan, Lila Howard, ? May, Veda Kingsley.

CHIPPENHAM CRICKET CLUB, either in John Coles Park or on the Town Ground.

WESTINGHOUSE CRICKET TEAM. Back row, from left: Alan Boyd, Alan Shepherd, -?-, ? Woodley, Fred Young, -?-, -?-, Laurence Church. Seated: Reg Sharpe, Luke Gale, -?-, Dick Townsend, -?-. This photograph was taken in the late 1930s.

CHIPPENHAM RUGBY CLUB, 1946/7. Back row, from left: -?-, Wilf Kirk, Reginald Baker, -?-, ? Malpass, -?-, -?-, ? Romain. Middle row: Bobby Barrett, Cyril Lewis, ? McKinnis, -?-, -?-. Front row: -?-, -?-.

WESTMEAD FOOTBALL TEAM. In the 1918/19 season they beat Stothert's at Bath and the 'Pick of Bath and District'. Several of the players went on to play for Chippenham Town and even represented the county.

ST PAUL'S FOOTBALL TEAM with the Revd Cornwall, probably in the late 1930s. Harold Evans is kneeling at the centre of the middle row.

ST PAUL'S SCHOOL FOOTBALL CLUB, possibly in the 1920s. Mr Thurston was headmaster.

CHIPPENHAM GRAMMAR SCHOOL FOOTBALL TEAM, 1936. Alex Cogswell is seated on the left of the middle row, in front of Mr Billy Gee, schoolmaster, and Jack Freegard is on the right sitting on the ground.

CHIPPENHAM GRAMMAR SCHOOL UNDER 14S RUGBY TEAM, 1966–7. Peter Shipway, front right, was serving with the Merchant Navy in Japan when he was tragically killed in an accident.

CHIPPENHAM UNITED ASSOCIATION FOOTBALL CLUB CUP WINNERS, 1905/6. Not all of these gentlemen were named on the photograph but those names that are known are as follows: Standing, far left: Mr S.A. Cook (chairman); sitting next to him is Mr P. Bunting, A. Bromley, W. Escott and A. Allen. The man with the towel over his shoulder is F. Hunt (trainer). Seated in the front, from the left are: A. Vennel, F. Beynon, R. Middle, W. Knight and A. Hazel.

MR JOHN BOYD came to play for Chippenham Town in 1948, from Newport County, after serving in the Royal Navy. This picture, taken to commemorate the team's success in 1951 in winning the Western League Cup, shows from the left, back row: John Boyd, Stan Titcombe, Alan Bates, Ronnie Haycock, Kenny Davis. Middle row: Bill Fowles (sec.), Roy Strange (trainer), George James, Jack Hamilton, George Osman, Vic Harris, Sid Kierney, Basil Marchant, Cecil Hemmings (trainer), Wilf Escott (sec.). Front row: Ray Escott (committee), Tom Price (chairman), Terry Milsom, George Flowe (MD), Ken Abrahams (captain), Tom Cruse (president), Ron Flower (director), ? Poulter (mascot). Chippenham went on to play Leyton Orient in the first round of the FA Cup; they were beaten 2 goals to 1.

DARTS CLUB WINNERS at Lacock Working Men's Club in the mid-1950s. From the left: Len Flower, ? Lydall, Sid Maslen, Bill Hindle, Jock Mc?, Fred Stevens presenting the cup to Ted Drewitt, Don Vines, Pete James, Colin Lovelock, Michael Potter, -?-, Tony Edwards.

LACOCK FOOTBALL TEAM, 1947/8.

LACOCK CRICKET TEAM, 1930. Standing, from left: Ivor Turner, Bert Stevens, Henry Barnes, ? Cleverly, D. Vines, George Selman, Dr Moore, George Gerrish. Crouching: umpire Billy Ball, Stan Pickford, Bob Hayward, Dick Hopkins, Wally Bird.

CHIPPENHAM AND DISTRICT SKITTLE LEAGUE, Lacock A Team, winners 1927/8, 1928/9, 1929/30. Mr Joseph is on the right hand side of the middle row.

SECTION TEN

Occasions

CHIPPENHAM LAND ARMY GIRLS in the Chippenham Hospital Victory Carnival. Betty Bailiff is driving the tractor.

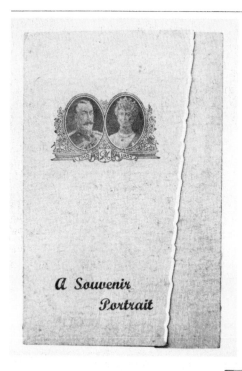

PUPIL'S SOUVENIR PHOTOGRAPH COVER, from Ivy Lane School, made to celebrate the Jubilee of King George V in 1935.

A Souvenir Portrait

Programme of Events :: May 6th, 1935

10 a.m.	THANKSGIVING SERVICE at the Cenotaph. (If wet, in the Parish Church).	
1 p.m.	CRICKET MATCH. Chippenham Town v. Westinghouse Brake & Signal Co., Ltd.	
3 p.m.	FOOTBALL MATCH. Chippenham Town v. Chippenham Rovers.	
3.45 p.m.	TEA for School Children.	
4 p.m.	TEA and CONCERT for People aged 70 and over and for Blind, at Constitutional Hall.	
4.30 p.m.	SCHOOL CHILDREN'S MARCH to John Coles Park.	
5.30 p.m.	SCHOOLS FOOTBALL and HOCKEY TOURNAMENTS in John Coles Park.	
7 p.m.	WHIST DRIVE at Town Hall. Proceeds in aid of King George V. Trust Fund.	
8.15 p.m.	CONCERT by British Legion Band in Market Place, followed by Dancing.	
9 p.m.	GRAND JUBILEE BALL in Neeld Hall. Proceeds to King George V. Trust Fund.	
9 p.m.	OPEN-AIR ENTERTAINMENT at Maud Heath Monument by Chippenham Boy Scouts.	
10 p.m.	LIGHTING OF CHAIN BONFIRE and FIREWORKS at Maud Heath Monument by Chippenham Boy Scouts.	

KING GEORGE V. JUBILEE TRUST FUND. His Worship the Mayor appeals for generous support to his Fund for the above.

THURSDAY, May 9th.

8.15 p.m.	GRAND JUBILEE VARIETY CONCERT by Chippenham Operatic & Dramatic Society in Neeld Hall. Popular prices. Proceeds in aid of King George V. Trust Fund.	

S. W. H. DANN, *Hon. Secretary.*

THE PROGRAMME OF EVENTS for the Jubilee celebrations for King George V in 1935. The proceeds of the celebrations were to go to the King's Trust Fund. The secretary was Mr S.W.H. Dann.

A 'MOTORKHANA' of decorated prams and scooters, organized for Chippenham's first Hospital Carnival which was held in John Coles Park around 1924. The costume most favoured by the young entrants appears to be that of the nurse.

RESIDENTS, from the Butts, Causeway and London Road area, celebrating the Coronation of HM King George VI in 1937. Mr and Mrs Dean, of the Store, are standing third and fourth from the left in the middle row. Mr Comely is in the back row, wearing the hat, and Mr Wheeler, who had one of the shops in the Causeway, is on the extreme right of the picture.

DOUGLAS AND RONALD SHIPWAY outside their home in Park Lane, which was decorated for the Coronation in 1937 of HM King George VI.

VICTORY CELEBRATIONS, in 1945, in Wood Lane, Chippenham, after the Second World War. Among those present were Janet Hawkins, Mary Cole, Mr Cole, Mrs Armstrong, Mrs Cole, Mr Sartin and Mr Walker.

VICTORY PARTY, held at Sheldon Road, to celebrate the end of the Second World War.

VICTORY PARTY held at Lowden School, Sheldon Road, at the end of the Second World War. Several ARP wardens were present.

VICTORY CELEBRATIONS, held in the sheds at Syms Transport Yard for the people of the area between The Three Crowns and The Royal Oak, including the courtyards off London Road which were known as Rural Gardens.

VE PARTY in Factory Lane, now called Westmead Lane. The cottages on the right are Westmead Cottages. Opposite these were more cottages and three slaughter houses. Avonside, which was a North Wilts Sheltered Scheme, stands there now. Behind the tree are houses in what was Blind Lane, off Gladstone Road. (Blind Lane was demolished when River Street was widened.) River Street Cottages, along with the Lamb Inn and the Wool Pack, have completely disappeared. Among those in the picture are Mrs Foyle, wearing the cap, Mrs Cadey, Mrs Comley and her sister Mrs Cord, Mrs Cook, who sold chips at the fountain in the Market Place, with her daughter Kitty Pringle of River Street, and Mrs Phillips with her son. Tony Beavis and John Comley are sitting in the foreground. Helping them to celebrate were the evacuees, who spent the war years in River Street and Factory Lane.

PROGRAMME to celebrate four hundred years of Chippenham's history. This was marked by an exhibition in the Town Hall in June 1954.

MR HUGHES was Managing Director of Westinghouse and Mayor of Chippenham in 1945. He is seen here with his wife at the coronation party held for the children of the Rural Garden district in 1953.

TO CELEBRATE THE CORONATION OF QUEEN ELIZABETH II in 1953 all the children in the Rural Gardens were given a Bible. Here, Mr Baker is presenting a Bible to the daughter of Iris Dolman in the presence of the Mayor of Chippenham, Mr Cruse.

CELEBRATIONS at Avonside, a North Wilts Sheltered Scheme in Westmead Lane, for the Jubilee of HM Queen Elizabeth II in 1977. Standing, from the left: Mrs Waite, Miss Iles, Mr Waite, Mrs Dean, Mrs Boyce, Mrs Kemp. Seated: Mrs Morgan, -?-, Mrs Warner, Mrs Peppin, -?-.

'BUFFALO' BILL CODY, whose circus visited Cocklebury Lane, Chippenham in the 1930s.

'BUFFALO' BILL CODY with some of the Indians who appeared in his travelling circus when it came to Cocklebury Lane, Chippenham.

ERNEST MCKENNA, dressed as Gordon Richards, the jockey, in the 1946 Chippenham Carnival. The donkey was owned by Gordon Self of Cocklebury Farm.

CHOIR BOYS David Parsons, Richard Parsons, Cecil Fenner and Patrick Heath escort the St Andrew's Church Guild entry in the 1949 Chippenham Carnival. The model of the church spire was constructed to encourage donations to the church funds.

CARNIVAL QUEEN'S FLOAT in the 1949/50 Chippenham Carnival, sponsored by Chippenham United Football Club.

ST ANDREW'S GUILD ENTRY, depicting Noah's Ark, is presented with the first prize certificate in the 1950 Chippenham Carnival. Jack Hart and Cecil Fenner, two of the choir boys, are on the left.

ST ANDREW'S HOSPITAL STAFF join with nurses from Frogwell Hospital for their entry in the Chippenham Carnival in the 1960s asking for 'Blood, 100% Alcohol'.

THE MONKTON HILL OPERATIC GROUP'S ENTRY in the Jubilee Carnival, 1977. The theme was 'In the Days of Good Queen Bess'.

CHRISTMAS PARTY held at the Butts Garage. The Butts are so named because they stand on the site of medieval archery butts.

DINNER AT THE WORKING MEN'S CLUB, Lacock. Sitting front left is Mr Joseph Vines, with Jack Wheeler and Fred Wheeler beside him. Across the table and from the right are Lena May, Mrs May and Charlie Everleigh.

A SCENE FAMILIAR IN LACOCK in the middle of the last century when, once or twice a year, dancing bears were led into the village, along with musicians and other entertainers. Old records tell how, if the handlers became drunk they would be locked up in the blind house for the night with their bears. This picture was taken for a pageant held in 1938/9, Bob Vines playing the part of the bear, and his brother Eric, the handler.

A FLOCK OF SHEEP wander gently through Lacock with only one motor car in sight, outside the Red Lion. Thankfully, apart from an increase in traffic, the village remains very much the same.

ACKNOWLEDGEMENTS

Mrs Andrews • Mr & Mrs Badminton • Mr & Mrs Baker • Mrs M. Baker
Mrs Bishop • Mr Boyd • Mr & Mrs Cleverley • Mr Drewett • Mrs Evans
Mr D. Evans • Mrs Faulkner • Mr Flower • Mrs P. Foster
The Revd C. Fowler • Mr & Mrs Freegard • Mrs Gilbert • Mrs Greenman
Mrs G. Harris • Mrs Hawkins • Mrs B. Howard • Miss Hunt • Mrs Loud
Mrs Love • Mrs Matthews • Mrs McGovern • Mrs Northover • Mr Roberts
Mr & Mrs Ryall • Mrs Shipway • Mrs M. Summers • Mr Tatum
Mr Thompson • Mr D. Vines • Mrs Yeomans • Mrs Young • Mrs P. Foster